A L

A Little Book of Bible Promises

Compiled by Richard A. Daly

Marshall Pickering
An Imprint of HarperCollins*Publishers*

This volume is dedicated to my wife, Maxine.

Marshall Pickering is an Imprint of
HarperCollins*Religious*
Part of HarperCollins*Publishers*
77-85 Fulham Palace Road, London W6 8JB

First published in Great Britain
in 1996 by Marshall Pickering

3 5 7 9 10 8 6 4 2

A catalogue record for this book is available from the British Library

ISBN 0 551 03020 8

Printed and bound in Great Britain by
Woolnough Bookbinding Ltd, Irthlingborough, Northamptonshire

A Little Book of Bible Promises

Introduction

Throughout the pages of the Bible you can find priceless gems of treasure just waiting to be discovered in the form of God's precious promises. These promises range from the assurance of strength and encouragement to hope and celebration in a God whose words never fail:

For no matter how many promises God has made, they are 'Yes' in Christ.

2 Corinthians 1:20 (NIV)

God's love for us far exceeds our human knowledge of understanding and because He cares for us so much, whatever circumstance we may find ourselves in, you can be assured that God does understand how you feel and He has a special promise just for you.

A Little Book of Bible Promises contains but a few of the thousands of promises that can be found throughout the scriptures. It is aimed to all who at times become beset by the daily pressures and burdens in life, who desire to seek a spiritual remedy specifically designed to meet their needs. It is hoped that by using biblical examples where such times were also experienced by God's people, and by supplying meaningful passages of scripture in the most favourable translation, that a form of identification with the experience and encouragement will be obtained by the reader.

Every one of you knows in his heart and soul that the Lord your God has given you all the good things that he promised. Every promise he has made has been kept; not one has failed.

Joshua 23:14 (GNB)

Richard A. Daly

When Feeling Afraid

And they rose up the same hour, and returned to Jerusalem, and found the eleven gathered together, and them that were with them, Saying, The Lord is risen indeed, and hath appeared to Simon. And they told what things were done in the way, and how he was known of them in breaking of bread. And as they thus spake, Jesus himself stood in the midst of them, and saith unto them, Peace be unto you. But they were terrified and affrightened, and supposed that they had seen a spirit.

Luke 4:33–37 (KJV)

Be strong and courageous. Do not be afraid or terrified because of them, for the Lord your God goes with you; he will never leave you nor forsake you.

Deuteronomy 31:6 (NIV)

But even if you should suffer for what is right, you are blessed. 'Do not fear what they fear; do not be frightened.' But in your hearts set Christ apart as Lord.

1 Peter 3:14–15 (NIV)

When I am afraid, I will trust in you. In God, whose word I praise, in God I trust; I will not be afraid. What can mortal man do to me?

Psalm 56:3–4 (NIV)

The Lord is my light and my salvation; I will fear no one. The Lord protects me from all danger; I will never be afraid.

Psalm 27:1 (GNB)

Have I not commanded you? Be strong and courageous. Do not be terrified; do not be discouraged, for the Lord your God will be with you wherever you go.

Joshua 1:9 (NIV)

Peace I leave with you, my peace I give unto you: not as the world giveth, give I unto you. Let not your heart be troubled, neither let it be afraid.

John 14:27 (KJV)

God is my saviour; I will trust him and not be afraid. The Lord gives me power and strength; he is my saviour.

Isaiah 12:2 (GNB)

What shall we then say to these things? If God be for us, who can be against us?

Romans 8:31 (KJV)

This is what the Lord says to you: 'Do not be afraid
or discouraged because of this vast army. For the
battle is not yours, but God's.'

2 Chronicles 20:15 (NIV)

So do not fear, for I am with you; do not be
dismayed, for I am your God. I will strengthen you
and help you; I will uphold you.

Isaiah 41:10 (NIV)

Do not be afraid, little flock, for your Father is
pleased to give you the kingdom.

Luke 12:32 (GNB)

For the Spirit that God has given you does not make
you slaves and cause you to be afraid; instead, the
Spirit makes you God's children, and by the Spirit's
power we cry out to God, 'Father! My Father!'

Romans 8:15 (GNB)

So we say with confidence, 'The Lord is my helper;
I will not be afraid. What can man do to me?'

Hebrews 13:6 (NIV)

For I am the Lord, your God, who takes hold of your
right hand and says to you, Do not fear; I will help
you.

Isaiah 41:13 (NIV)

Have no fear of sudden disaster or of the ruin that
overtakes the wicked, for the Lord will be your
confidence and will keep your foot from being
snared.

Proverbs 3:25–26 (NIV)

For God hath not given us the spirit of fear; but of
power, and of love, and of a sound mind.

2 Timothy 1:7 (KJV)

For the eyes of the Lord are over the righteous, and his ears are open unto their prayers: but the face of the Lord is against them that do evil.

1 Peter 3:12 (KJV)

And who is he that will harm you, if ye be followers of that which is good? But and if ye suffer for righteousness' sake, happy are ye: and be not afraid of their terror, neither be troubled...

1 Peter 3:13–14 (KJV)

When You are Angry

Now his elder son was in the field: and as he came and drew nigh to the house, he heard musick and dancing. And he called one of the servants, and asked what these things meant. And he said unto him, Thy brother is come; and thy father hath killed the fatted calf, because he hath received him safe and sound. And he was angry, and would not go in...

Luke 15:25—28 (KJV)

Then they cried out to the Lord in their trouble, and he brought them out of their distress. He stilled the storm to a whisper; the waves of the sea were hushed.

Psalm 107:28—29 (NIV)

I have told you these things, so that in me you may have peace. In this world you will have trouble. But take heart! I have overcome the world.

John 16:33 (NIV)

... for everyone born of God overcomes the world. This is the victory that has overcome the world, even our faith.

1 John 5:4 (NIV)

... thou art a God ready to pardon, gracious and merciful, slow to anger, and of great kindness ...

Nehemiah 9:17 (KJV)

His anger lasts only a moment, his goodness for a lifetime. Tears may flow in the night, but joy comes in the morning.

Psalm 30:5 (GNB)

Let all bitterness, and wrath, and anger, and
clamour, and evil speaking, be put away from you,
with all malice: And be ye kind one to another,
tenderhearted, forgiving one another, even as God
for Christ's sake hath forgiven you.

Ephesians 4:31–32 (KJV)

Dearly beloved, avenge not yourselves, but rather
give place unto wrath: for it is written, Vengeance is
mine; I will repay, saith the Lord. Therefore if thine
enemy hunger, feed him; if he thirst, give him
drink: for in so doing thou shalt heap coals of fire on
his head. Be not overcome of evil, but overcome evil
with good.

Romans 12:19–21 (KJV)

Wherefore, my beloved brethren, let every man be swift to hear, slow to speak, slow to wrath: For the wrath of man worketh not the righteousness of God.

James 1:19–20 (KJV)

To Those Experiencing Bereavement

And the king was much moved, and went up to the chamber over the gate, and wept: and as he went, thus he said, O my son Absalom, my son, my son Absalom! would God I had died for thee, O Absalom, my son, my son!

2 Samuel 18:33 (KJV)

Yea, though I walk through the valley of the shadow of death, I will fear no evil: for thou art with me; thy rod and thy staff they comfort me.

Psalm 23:4 (KJV)

My flesh and my heart faileth: but God is the strength of my heart, and my portion for ever.

Psalm 73:26 (KJV)

For God so loved the world, that he gave his only begotten Son, that whosoever believeth in him should not perish, but have everlasting life.

John 3:16 (KJV)

For I am certain that nothing can separate us from his love: neither death nor life, neither angels nor other heavenly rulers or powers, neither the present nor the future, neither the world above nor the world below — there is nothing in all creation that will ever be able to separate us from the love of God which is ours through Christ Jesus our Lord.

Romans 8:38–39 (GNB)

The wicked is driven away in his wickedness: but the righteous hath hope in his death.

Proverbs 14:32 (KJV)

For this God is our God for ever and ever: he will be our guide even unto death.

Psalm 48:14 (KJV)

He will swallow up death in victory; and the Lord God will wipe away tears from off all faces; and the rebuke of his people shall he take away from off all the earth: for the Lord hath spoken it.

Isaiah 25:8 (KJV)

... weeping may endure for a night, but joy cometh in the morning.

Psalm 30:5 (KJV)

Forasmuch then as the children are partakers of flesh and blood, he also himself likewise took part of the same; that through death he might destroy him that had the power of death, that is, the devil; And deliver them who through fear of death were all their lifetime subject to bondage.

Hebrews 2:14–15 (KJV)

But God will redeem my soul from the power of the grave: for he shall receive me.

Psalm 49:15 (KJV)

I will ransom them from the power of the grave; I will redeem them from death: O death, I will be thy plagues; O grave, I will be thy destruction: repentance shall be hid from mine eyes.

Hosea 13:14 (KJV)

In Times of Celebration

And he arose, and came to his father. But when he was yet a great
way off, his father saw him, and had compassion, and ran, and fell
on his neck, and kissed him. And the son said unto him, Father,
I have sinned against heaven, and in thy sight, and am no more
worthy to be called thy son. But the father said to his servants,
Bring forth the best robe, and put it on him; and put a ring on his
hand, and shoes on his feet: And bring hither the fatted calf, and
kill it; and let us eat, and be merry: For this my son was dead, and
is alive again; he was lost, and is found. And they began to be
merry.

Luke 15:20−24 (KJV)

Happy is he that hath the God of Jacob for his help,
whose hope is in the Lord his God ...

Psalm 146:5 (KJV)

Let the heavens be glad, and let the earth rejoice: and let men say among the nations, The Lord reigneth.

1 Chronicles 16:31 (KJV)

I will be glad and rejoice in thee: I will sing praise to thy name, O thou most High.

Psalm 9:2 (KJV)

But I trust in your unfailing love; my heart rejoices in your salvation.

Psalm 13:5 (NIV)

We will rejoice in thy salvation, and in the name of our God we will set up our banners: the Lord fulfil all thy petitions.

Psalm 20:5 (KJV)

I will exalt you, O Lord, for you lifted me out of the depths and did not let my enemies gloat over me.

Psalm 30:1 (NIV)

Be glad in the Lord, and rejoice, ye righteous: and shout for joy, all ye that are upright in heart.

Psalm 32:11 (KJV)

But may all who seek you rejoice and be glad in you; may those who love your salvation always say, 'Let God be exalted!'

Psalm 70:4 (NIV)

My lips shall greatly rejoice when I sing unto thee; and my soul, which thou hast redeemed.

Psalm 71:23 (KJV)

Let the heavens rejoice, and let the earth be glad; let the sea roar, and the fulness thereof.

Psalm 96:11 (KJV)

Glory ye in his holy name: let the heart of them rejoice that seek the Lord.

Psalm 105:3 (KJV)

And it shall be said in that day, Lo, this is our God; we have waited for him, and he will save us: this is the Lord; we have waited for him, we will be glad and rejoice in his salvation.

Isaiah 25:9 (KJV)

The meek also shall increase their joy in the Lord, and the poor among men shall rejoice in the Holy One of Israel.

Isaiah 29:19 (KJV)

Fear not, O land; be glad and rejoice: for the Lord will do great things.

Joel 2:21 (KJV)

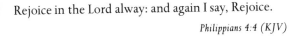

Rejoice in the Lord alway: and again I say, Rejoice.

Philippians 4:4 (KJV)

But rejoice, inasmuch as ye are partakers of Christ's suffering; that, when his glory shall be revealed, ye may be glad also with exceeding joy.

1 Peter 4:13 (KJV)

The righteous shall be glad in the Lord, and shall trust in him; and all the upright in heart shall glory.

Psalm 64:10 (KJV)

Satisfy us in the morning with your unfailing love, that we may sing for joy and be glad all our days.

Psalm 90:14 (NIV)

When in Need of Courage

Gideon replied, 'But Lord, how can I rescue Israel? My clan is the weakest in the tribe of Manasseh, and I am the least important member of my family.'

Judges 6:15 (GNB)

Be strong and of a good courage, fear not, nor be afraid of them: for the Lord thy God, he it is that doth go with thee; he will not fail thee, nor forsake thee.

Deuteronomy 31:6 (KJV)

And he gave Joshua the son of Nun a charge, and said, Be strong and of a good courage: for thou shalt bring the children of Israel into the land which I sware unto them: and I will be with thee.

Deuteronomy 31:23 (KJV)

Then shalt thou prosper, if thou takest heed to fulfil the statutes and judgments which the Lord charged Moses with concerning Israel: be strong, and of good courage; dread not, nor be dismayed.

1 Chronicles 22:13 (KJV)

And David said to Solomon his son, Be strong and of good courage, and do it: fear not, nor be dismayed: for the Lord God, even my God, will be with thee; he will not fail thee, nor forsake thee, until thou hast finished all the work for the service of the house of the Lord.

1 Chronicles 28:20 (KJV)

Wait on the Lord: be of good courage, and he shall strengthen thine heart: wait, I say, on the Lord.

Psalm 27:14 (KJV)

Be of good courage, and he shall strengthen your heart, all ye that hope in the Lord.

Psalm 31:24 (KJV)

Be ye strong therefore, and let not your hands be weak: for your work shall be rewarded.

2 Chronicles 15:7 (KJV)

Who is this King of glory? The Lord strong and mighty, the Lord mighty in battle.

Psalm 24:8 (KJV)

O Lord God Almighty, who is like you? You are mighty, O Lord, and your faithfulness surrounds you.

Psalm 89:8 (NIV)

The name of the Lord is a strong tower: the
righteous runneth into it, and is safe.

Proverbs 18:10 (KJV)

I will seek that which was lost, and bring again that
which was driven away, and will bind up that which
was broken, and will strengthen that which was sick:
but I will destroy the fat and the strong; I will feed
them with judgment.

Ezekiel 34:16 (KJV)

Therefore I take pleasure in infirmities, in
reproaches, in necessities, in persecutions, in
distresses for Christ's sake: for when I am weak, then
am I strong.

2 Corinthians 12:10 (KJV)

Finally, my brethren, be strong in the Lord, and in
the power of his might.

Ephesians 6:10 (KJV)

23

When Feeling Hurt

And when Esau heard the words of his father, he cried with a great and exceeding bitter cry, and said unto his father, Bless me, even me also, O my father. And he said, Thy brother came with subtilty, and hath taken away thy blessing.

Genesis 27:34–35 (KJV)

Praise be to the God and Father of our Lord Jesus Christ, the Father of compassion and the God of all comfort, who comforts us in all our troubles, so that we can comfort those in any trouble with the comfort we ourselves have received from God.

2 Corinthians 1:3–4 (NIV)

He that dwelleth in the secret place of the most
High shall abide under the shadow of the Almighty.
I will say of the Lord, He is my refuge and my
fortress: my God; in him will I trust.

Psalm 91:1–2 (KJV)

Yea, though I walk through the valley of the shadow
of death, I will fear no evil: for thou art with me; thy
rod and thy staff they comfort me.

Psalm 23:4 (KJV)

But Jesus turned him about, and when he saw her,
he said, Daughter, be of good comfort; thy faith
hath made thee whole.

Matthew 9:22 (KJV)

Cast thy burden upon the Lord, and he shall sustain
thee: he shall never suffer the righteous to be
moved.

Psalm 55:22 (KJV)

25

Come unto me, all ye that labour and are heavy
laden, and I will give you rest.

Matthew 11:28 (KJV)

God is our refuge and strength, a very present help
in trouble. Therefore will not we fear, though the
earth be removed, and though the mountains be
carried into the midst of the sea; Though the waters
thereof roar and be troubled, though the mountains
shake with the swelling thereof.

Psalm 46:1–3 (KJV)

The Lord is my rock, my fortress and my deliverer;
my God is my rock, in whom I take refuge. He is my
shield and the horn of my salvation, my stronghold.

Psalm 18:2 (NIV)

In Feelings of Failure

And the Lord turned, and looked upon Peter. And Peter remembered the word of the Lord, how he said unto him, Before the cock crow, thou shalt deny me thrice. And Peter went out, and wept bitterly.

Luke 22:61–62 (KJV)

Now I am about to go the way of all the earth. You know with all your heart and soul that not one of all the good promises the Lord your God gave you has failed. Every promise has been fulfilled; not one has failed.

Joshua 23:14 (NIV)

Praise be to the Lord, who has given rest to his people Israel just as he promised. Not one word has failed of all the good promises he gave through his servant Moses.

1 Kings 8:56 (NIV)

Now we pray to God that you will not do anything wrong. Not that people will see that we have stood the test but that you will do what is right even though we may seem to have failed.

2 Corinthians 13:7 (NIV)

My mind and my body may grow weak, but God is my strength; he is all I ever need.

Psalm 73:26 (GNB)

And the Lord thy God will make thee plenteous in
every work of thine hand, in the fruit of thy body,
and in the fruit of thy cattle, and in the fruit of thy
land, for good: for the Lord will again rejoice over
thee for good, as he rejoiced over thy fathers ...

Deuteronomy 30:9 (KJV)

Every man also to whom God hath given riches and
wealth, and hath given him power to eat thereof,
and to take his portion, and to rejoice in his labour;
this is the gift of God.

Ecclesiastes 5:19 (KJV)

That everyone may eat and drink, and find
satisfaction in all his toil – this is the gift of God.

Ecclesiastes 3:13 (NIV)

You will succeed in all you do, and light will shine
on your path.

Job 22:28 (GNB)

With me are riches and honor, enduring wealth and prosperity. My fruit is better than fine gold; what I yield surpasses choice silver.

Proverbs 8:18–19 (NIV)

When anyone is joined to Christ, he is a new being; the old is gone, the new has come.

2 Corinthians 5:17 (GNB)

I will cleanse them from all the sin they have committed against me and will forgive all their sins of rebellion against me.

Jeremiah 33:8 (NIV)

Regarding His Faithfulness

It was faith that made Abraham obey when God called him to go out to a country which God had promised to give him. He left his own country without knowing where he was going.

Hebrews 11:8 (GNB)

God is not a man, that he should lie, nor a son of man, that he should change his mind. Does he speak and then not act? Does he promise and not fulfill?

Numbers 23:19 (NIV)

For the promise is unto you, and to your children, and to all that are afar off, even as many as the Lord our God shall call.

Acts 2:39 (KJV)

But in keeping with his promise we are looking forward to a new heaven and a new earth, the home of righteousness.

2 Peter 3:13 (NIV)

Not one of all the Lord's good promises to the house of Israel failed; every one was fulfilled.

Joshua 21:45 (NIV)

For the sake of your servant and according to your will, you have done this great thing and made known all these great promises.

1 Chronicles 17:19 (NIV)

I will listen to what God the Lord will say; he promises peace to his people, his saints – but let them not return to folly.

Psalm 85:8 (NIV)

Your kingdom is an everlasting kingdom, and your dominion endures through all generations. The Lord is faithful to all his promises and loving toward all he has made.

Psalm 145:13 (NIV)

For no matter how many promises God has made, they are 'Yes' in Christ.

2 Corinthians 1:20 (NIV)

Lord God Almighty, none is as mighty as you; in all things you are faithful, O Lord.

Psalm 89:8 (GNB)

Your faithfulness continues through all generations; you established the earth, and it endures.

Psalm 119:90 (NIV)

It is a good thing to give thanks unto the Lord, and to sing praises unto thy name, O most High: To shew forth thy lovingkindness in the morning, and thy faithfulness every night ...

Psalm 92:1–2 (KJV)

The Lord's unfailing love and mercy still continue, Fresh as the morning, as sure as the sunrise.

Lamentations 3:22–23 (GNB)

Blessed is he whose help is the God of Jacob, whose hope is in the Lord his God, the Maker of heaven and earth, the sea, and everything in them – the Lord, who remains faithful forever.

Psalm 146:5–6 (NIV)

But Christ is faithful as a son over God's house. And we are his house, if we hold on to our courage and the hope of which we boast.

Hebrews 3:6 (NIV)

For Families

And the Lord God caused a deep sleep to fall upon Adam, and he slept: and he took one of his ribs, and closed up the flesh instead thereof; And the rib, which the Lord God had taken from man, made he a woman, and brought her unto the man. And Adam said, This is now bone of my bones, and flesh of my flesh: she shall be called Woman, because she was taken out of Man. Therefore shall a man leave his father and his mother, and shall cleave unto his wife: and they shall be one flesh.

Genesis 2:21–24 (KJV)

Children's children are a crown to the aged, and parents are the pride of their children.

Proverbs 17:6 (NIV)

Who can find a virtuous woman? for her price is far above rubies. The heart of her husband doth safely trust in her, so that he shall have no need of spoil. She will do him good and not evil all the days of her life. Her children arise up, and call her blessed; her husband also, and he praiseth her.

Proverbs 31:10–12,28 (KJV)

Husbands, in the same way be considerate as you live with your wives, and treat them with respect as the weaker partner and as heirs with you of the gracious gift of life, so that nothing will hinder your prayers.

1 Peter 3:7 (NIV)

Blessed is every one that feareth the Lord; that walketh in his ways…Thy wife shall be as a fruitful vine by the sides of thine house: thy children like olive plants round about thy table.

Psalm 128:1,3 (KJV)

House and riches are the inheritance of fathers: and a prudent wife is from the Lord.

Proverbs 19:14 (KJV)

Whoso findeth a wife findeth a good thing, and obtaineth favour of the Lord.

Proverbs 18:22 (KJV)

Live joyfully with the wife whom thou lovest all the days of the life of thy vanity, which he hath given thee under the sun, all the days of thy vanity: for that is thy portion in this life, and in thy labour which thou takest under the sun.

Ecclesiastes 9:9 (KJV)

Let thy fountain be blessed: and rejoice with the wife of thy youth. Let her be as the loving hind and pleasant roe; let her breasts satisfy thee at all times; and be thou ravished always with her love.

Proverbs 5:18–19 (KJV)

Children are a gift from the Lord; they are a real blessing.

Psalm 127:3 (GNB)

See that you don't despise any of these little ones. Their angels in heaven, I tell you, are always in the presence of my Father in heaven.

Matthew 18:10 (GNB)

Then little children were brought to Jesus for him to place his hands on them and pray for them. But the disciples rebuked those who brought them. Jesus said, 'Let the little children come to me, and do not hinder them, for the kingdom of heaven belongs to such as these.'

Matthew 19:13–14 (NIV)

And all thy children shall be taught of the Lord; and great shall be the peace of thy children.

Isaiah 54:13 (KJV)

Train up a child in the way he should go: and when he is old, he will not depart from it.

Proverbs 22:6 (KJV)

And Jesus called a little child unto him, and set him in the midst of them, And said, Verily I say unto you, Except ye be converted, and become as little children, ye shall not enter into the kingdom of heaven. Whosoever therefore shall humble himself as this little child, the same is greatest in the kingdom of heaven.

Matthew 18:2–4 (KJV)

My son, attend to my words; incline thine ear unto my sayings. Let them not depart from thine eyes; keep them in the midst of thine heart. For they are life unto those that find them, and health to all their flesh.

Proverbs 4:20–22 (KJV)

Listen, my son, accept what I say, and the years of
your life will be many. I guide you in the way of
wisdom and lead you along straight paths. When
you walk, your steps will not be hampered; when
you run, you will not stumble. Hold on to
instruction, do not let it go; guard it well, for it is
your life.

Proverbs 4:10–13 (NIV)

Sovereign Lord, I put my hope in you; I have trusted
in you since I was young.

Psalm 71:5 (GNB)

Don't let anyone look down on you because you are
young, but set an example for the believers in
speech, in life, in love, in faith and in purity.

1 Timothy 4:12 (NIV)

When You Need Forgiveness

Have mercy upon me, O God, according to thy lovingkindness:
according unto the multitude of thy tender mercies blot out my
transgressions. Wash me throughly from mine iniquity, and cleanse
me from my sin.

Psalm 51:1–2 (KJV)

Come now, and let us reason together, saith the
Lord: though your sins be as scarlet, they shall be as
white as snow; though they be red like crimson,
they shall be as wool.

Isaiah 1:18 (KJV)

I will heal their backsliding, I will love them freely:
for mine anger is turned away from him.

Hosea 14:4 (KJV)

Bless the Lord, O my soul, and forget not all his benefits: Who forgiveth all thine iniquities; who healeth all thy diseases; Who redeemeth thy life from destruction; who crowneth thee with lovingkindness and tender mercies...

Psalm 103:2–4 (KJV)

All the prophets testify about him that everyone who believes in him receives forgiveness of sins through his name.

Acts 10:43 (NIV)

In him we have redemption through his blood, the forgiveness of sins, in accordance with the riches of God's grace...

Ephesians 1:7 (NIV)

If my people, which are called by my name, shall humble themselves, and pray, and seek my face, and turn from their wicked ways; then will I hear from heaven, and will forgive their sin, and will heal their land.

2 Chronicles 7:14 (KJV)

For thou, Lord, art good, and ready to forgive; and plenteous in mercy unto all them that call upon thee.

Psalm 86:5 (KJV)

If you forgive others the wrongs they have done to you, your Father in heaven will also forgive you.

Matthew 6:14 (GNB)

If we confess our sins, he is faithful and just to forgive us our sins, and to cleanse us from all unrighteousness.

1 John 1:9 (KJV)

When You Need Guidance

And Philip ran thither to him, and heard him read the prophet
Esaias, and said, Understandest thou what thou readest? And he
said, How can I, except some man should guide me? And he
desired Philip that he would come up and sit with him.

Acts 8:30–31 (KJV)

The Lord will guide you always; he will satisfy your
needs in a sun-scorched land and will strengthen
your frame. You will be like a well-watered garden,
like a spring whose waters never fail.

Isaiah 58:11 (NIV)

Faithful to your promise, you led the people you had rescued; by your strength you guided them to your sacred land.

Exodus 15:13 (GNB)

Because of your great compassion you did not abandon them in the desert. By day the pillar of cloud did not cease to guide them on their path, nor the pillar of fire by night to shine on the way they were to take. You gave your good Spirit to instruct them. You did not withhold your manna from their mouths, and you gave them water for their thirst.

Nehemiah 9:19–20 (NIV)

This God is our God for ever and ever; he will lead us for all time to come.

Psalm 48:14 (GNB)

Where can I go from your Spirit? Where can I flee from your presence? If I go up to the heavens, you are there; if I make my bed in the depths, you are there. If I rise on the wings of the dawn, if I settle on the far side of the sea, even there your hand will guide me, your right hand will hold me fast.

Psalm 139:7–10 (NIV)

I guide you in the way of wisdom and lead you along straight paths.

Proverbs 4:11 (NIV)

But when he, the Spirit of truth, comes, he will guide you into all truth. He will not speak on his own; he will speak only what he hears, and he will tell you what is yet to come.

John 16:13 (NIV)

You guide me with your instruction and at the end you will recieve me with honour.

Psalm 73:24 (GNB)

I will lead the blind by ways they have not known, along unfamiliar paths I will guide them; I will turn the darkness into light before them and make the rough places smooth...

Isaiah 42:16 (NIV)

Regarding Healing

And lest I should be exalted above measure through the abundance of the revelations, there was given to me a thorn in the flesh, the messenger of Satan to buffet me, lest I should be exalted above measure. For this thing I besought the Lord thrice, that it might depart from me.

2 Corinthians 12:7–8 (KJV)

But he was wounded for our transgressions, he was bruised for our iniquities: the chastisement of our peace was upon him; and with his stripes we are healed.

Isaiah 53:5 (KJV)

And when he was come into the house, the blind men came to him: and Jesus saith unto them, Believe ye that I am able to do this? They said unto him, Yea, Lord. Then touched he their eyes, saying, According to your faith be it unto you. And their eyes were opened…

Matthew 9:28–30 (KJV)

Heal me, O Lord, and I shall be healed; save me, and I shall be saved: for thou art my praise.

Jeremiah 17:14 (KJV)

And ye shall serve the Lord your God, and he shall bless thy bread, and thy water; and I will take sickness away from the midst of thee.

Exodus 23:25 (KJV)

'I will go and make him well,' Jesus said.

Matthew 8:7 (GNB)

Nevertheless, I will bring health and healing to it;
I will heal my people and will let them enjoy
abundant peace and security.

Jeremiah 33:6 (NIV)

Is any sick among you? let him call for the elders of
the church; and let them pray over him, anointing
him with oil in the name of the Lord: And the
prayer of faith shall save the sick, and the Lord shall
raise him up; and if he have committed sins, they
shall be forgiven him. Confess your faults one to
another, and pray one for another, that ye may be
healed. The effectual fervent prayer of a righteous
man availeth much.

James 5:14–16 (KJV)

For I will restore health unto thee, and I will heal
thee of thy wounds, saith the Lord...

Jeremiah 30:17 (KJV)

God Hears

Hear, O Lord, when I cry with my voice: have mercy also upon me, and answer me. Hide not thy face far from me...put not thy servant away in anger; thou hast been my help; leave me not, neither forsake me, O God of my salvation.

Psalm 27:7,9 (KJV)

Call unto me, and I will answer thee, and shew thee great and mighty things, which thou knowest not.

Jeremiah 33:3 (KJV)

In my distress I called upon the Lord, and cried to my God: and he did hear my voice out of his temple, and my cry did enter into his ears.

2 Samuel 22:7 (KJV)

Lord, thou hast heard the desire of the humble:
thou wilt prepare their heart, thou wilt cause thine
ear to hear…

Psalm 10:17 (KJV)

I have called upon thee, for thou wilt hear me,
O God: incline thine ear unto me, and hear my
speech.

Psalm 17:6 (KJV)

Surely the arm of the Lord is not too short to save,
nor his ear too dull to hear.

Isaiah 59:1 (NIV)

Even before they finish praying to me, I will answer
their prayers.

Isaiah 65:24 (GNB)

Praise be to the Lord, who has given rest to his people Israel just as he promised. Not one word has failed of all the good promises he gave through his servant Moses.

1 Kings 8:56 (NIV)

The Lord is not slow in keeping his promise, as some understand slowness. He is patient with you, not wanting anyone to perish, but everyone to come to repentance.

2 Peter 3:9 (NIV)

God is not a man, that he should lie; neither the son of man, that he should repent: hath he said, and shall he not do it? or hath he spoken, and shall he not make it good?

Numbers 23:19 (KJV)

For the people shall dwell in Zion at Jerusalem:
thou shalt weep no more: he will be very gracious
unto thee at the voice of thy cry; when he shall hear
it, he will answer thee.

Isaiah 30:19 (KJV)

Then shall ye call upon me, and ye shall go and pray
unto me, and I will hearken unto you.

Jeremiah 29:12 (KJV)

The Lord is nigh unto all them that call upon him,
to all that call upon him in truth. He will fulfil the
desire of them that fear him: he also will hear their
cry, and will save them.

Psalm 145:18–19 (KJV)

In Times of Joy

The angel said to the women, 'Do not be afraid, for I know that you are looking for Jesus, who was crucified. He is not here; he has risen, just as he said. Come and see the place where he lay. Then go quickly and tell his disciples. . .' So the women hurried away from the tomb, afraid yet filled with joy. .:

Matthew 28:5−8 (NIV)

For God giveth to a man that is good in his sight wisdom, and knowledge, and joy...

Ecclesiastes 2:26 (KJV)

Be glad in the Lord, and rejoice, ye righteous: and shout for joy, all ye that are upright in heart.

Psalm 32:11 (KJV)

Restore unto me the joy of thy salvation; and
uphold me with thy free spirit.

Psalm 51:12 (KJV)

Once more the humble will rejoice in the Lord; the
needy will rejoice in the Holy One of Israel.

Isaiah 29:19 (NIV)

Therefore the redeemed of the Lord shall return,
and come with singing unto Zion; and everlasting
joy shall be upon their head: they shall obtain
gladness and joy; and sorrow and mourning shall
flee away.

Isaiah 35:10–11 (KJV)

Yet I will rejoice in the Lord, I will joy in the God of
my salvation.

Habakkuk 3:18 (KJV)

And the angel said unto them, Fear not: for, behold,
I bring you good tidings of great joy, which shall be
to all people. For unto you is born this day in the
city of David a Saviour, which is Christ the Lord.

Luke 2:10–11 (KJV)

Make me to hear joy and gladness; that the bones
which thou hast broken may rejoice.

Psalm 51:8 (KJV)

I tell you that in the same way there will be more
rejoicing in heaven over one sinner who repents
than over ninety-nine righteous persons who do
not need to repent.

Luke 15:7 (NIV)

I have told you this so that my joy may be in you
and that your joy may be complete.

John 15:11 (NIV)

A woman giving birth to a child has pain because her time has come; but when her baby is born she forgets the anguish because of her joy that a child is born into the world. So with you: Now is your time of grief, but I will see you again and you will rejoice, and no one will take away your joy.

John 16:21–22 (NIV)

I am coming to you now, but I say these things while I am still in the world, so that they may have the full measure of my joy within them.

John 17:13 (NIV)

You have made known to me the paths of life; you will fill me with joy in your presence.

Acts 2:28 (NIV)

They that sow in tears shall reap in joy.

Psalm 126:5 (KJV)

May the God of hope fill you with all joy and peace as you trust in him, so that you may overflow with hope by the power of the Holy Spirit.

Romans 15:13 (NIV)

But rejoice that you participate in the sufferings of Christ, so that you may be overjoyed when his glory is revealed.

1 Peter 4:13 (NIV)

And these things write we unto you, that your joy may be full.

1 John 1:4 (KJV)

Now unto him that is able to keep you from falling, and to present you faultless before the presence of his glory with exceeding joy...

Jude 1:24 (KJV)

To Those who are Lonely

That night Jacob got up and took his two wives, his two
maidservants and his eleven sons and crossed the ford of the
Jabbok. And after he had sent them across the stream, he sent over
all his possessions. So Jacob was left alone . . .

Genesis 32:22–24 (NIV)

Where can I go from your spirit? Where can I flee
from your presence? If I go up to the heavens, you
are there; if I make my bed in the depths, you are
there. If I rise on the wings of the dawn, if I settle on
the far side of the sea, even there your hand will
guide me, your right hand will hold me fast.

Psalm 139:7–10 (NIV)

I am always aware of the Lord's presence; he is near, and nothing can shake me.

Psalm 16:8 (GNB)

So do not fear, for I am with you; do not be dismayed, for I am your God. I will strengthen you and help you; I will uphold you with my righteous right hand.

Isaiah 41:10 (NIV)

And the Lord, he it is that doth go before thee; he will be with thee, he will not fail thee, neither forsake thee: fear not, neither be dismayed.

Deuteronomy 31:8 (KJV)

I will not leave you comfortless: I will come to you.

John 14:18 (KJV)

For God has said, 'I will never leave you; I will never abandon you.' Let us be bold, then, and say, 'The Lord is my helper, I will not be afraid. What can anyone do to me?'

Hebrews 13:5–6 (GNB)

He did this so that they would look for him, and perhaps find him as they felt about for him. Yet God is actually not far from any one of us; as someone has said, 'In him we live and move and exist.'

Acts 17:27 (GNB)

Then shalt thou call, and the Lord shall answer; thou shalt cry, and he shall say, Here I am...

Isaiah 58:9 (KJV)

And, behold, I am with thee, and will keep thee in all places whither thou goest, and will bring thee again into this land; for I will not leave thee, until I have done that which I have spoken to thee of.

Genesis 28:15 (KJV)

Regarding Long Life

Turn again, and tell Hezekiah the captain of my people, Thus saith the Lord, the God of David thy father, I have heard thy prayer, I have seen thy tears: behold, I will heal thee: on the third day thou shalt go up unto the house of the Lord. And I will add unto thy days fifteen years...

2 Kings 20:5–6 (KJV)

Is not wisdom found among the aged? Does not long life bring understanding? To God belong wisdom and power; counsel and understanding are his.

Job 12:12–13 (NIV)

Children's children are a crown to the aged, and parents are the pride of their children.

Proverbs 17:6 (NIV)

The glory of young men is their strength: and the beauty of old men is the gray head.

Proverbs 20:29 (KJV)

Even to your old age and gray hairs I am he, I am he who will sustain you. I have made you and I will carry you; I will sustain you and I will rescue you.

Isaiah 46:4 (NIV)

Do not cast me away when I am old; do not forsake me when my strength is gone.

Psalm 71:9 (NIV)

Walk in all the way that the Lord your God has commanded you, so that you may live and prosper and prolong your days in the land that you will possess.

Deuteronomy 5:33 (NIV)

Don't forget what I teach you, my son. Always remember what I tell you to do. My teaching will give you a long and prosperous life.

Proverbs 3:1–2 (GNB)

Respect your father and your mother, so that you may live a long time in the land that I am giving you.

Exodus 20:12 (GNB)

He shall call upon me, and I will answer him: I will be with him in trouble; I will deliver him, and honour him. With long life will I satisfy him, and shew him my salvation.

Psalm 91:15–16 (KJV)

Regarding His Love

He saith unto him the third time,
Simon, son of Jonas, lovest thou me?

John 21:17 (KJV)

Give thanks to the Lord, because he is good; his love is eternal.

1 Chronicles 16:34 (GNB)

But God commendeth his love toward us, in that, while we were yet sinners, Christ died for us.

Romans 5:8 (KJV)

The Lord thy God in the midst of thee is mighty; he
will save, he will rejoice over thee with joy; he will
rest in his love, he will joy over thee with singing.

Zephaniah 3:17 (KJV)

The Lord says 'I will bring my people back to me.
I will love them with all my heart...'

Hosea 14:4 (GNB)

Jesus answered and said unto him, If a man love me,
he will keep my words: and my Father will love him,
and we will come unto him, and make our abode
with him.

John 14:23 (KJV)

Greater love hath no man than this, that a man lay
down his life for his friends.

John 15:13 (KJV)

Who shall separate us from the love of Christ? shall tribulation, or distress, or persecution, or famine, or nakedness, or peril, or sword?

Romans 8:35 (KJV)

Behold, what manner of love the Father hath bestowed upon us, that we should be called the sons of God: therefore the world knoweth us not, because it knew him not.

1 John 3:1 (KJV)

He that loveth not knoweth not God; for God is love.

1 John 4:8 (KJV)

Herein is love, not that we loved God, but that he loved us, and sent his Son to be the propitiation for our sins.

1 John 4:10 (KJV)

No man hath seen God at any time. If we love one another, God dwelleth in us, and his love is perfected in us.

1 John 4:12 (KJV)

And he passed in front of Moses, proclaiming, 'The Lord, the Lord, the compassionate and gracious God, slow to anger, abounding in love and faithfulness…'

Exodus 34:6 (NIV)

How priceless is your unfailing love! Both high and low among men find refuge in the shadow of your wings.

Psalm 36:7 (NIV)

May your constant love be with us, Lord, as we put our hope in you.

Psalm 33:22 (GNB)

But I am like an olive tree flourishing in the house of God; I trust in God's unfailing love for ever and ever.

Psalm 52:8 (NIV)

Your constant love reaches the heavens; your faithfulness touches the skies.

Psalm 57:10 (GNB)

How great is your constant love for me! You have saved me from the grave itself.

Psalm 86:13 (GNB)

Give thanks to the God of heaven; His love is eternal.

Psalm 136:26 (GNB)

For I, the Lord, love justice; I hate robbery and iniquity. In my faithfulness I will reward them and make an everlasting covenant with them.

Isaiah 61:8 (NIV)

In all their distress he too was distressed, and the angel of his presence saved them. In his love and mercy he redeemed them; he lifted them up and carried them all the days of old.

Isaiah 63:9 (NIV)

Because of the Lord's great love we are not consumed, for his compassions never fail.

Lamentations 3:22 (NIV)

For God so loved the world that he gave his one and only Son, that whoever believes in him shall not perish but have eternal life.

John 3:16 (NIV)

For Help to Overcome

I don't do the good I want to do; instead, I do the evil that I do not want to do. If I do what I don't want to do, this means that I am no longer the one who does it; instead, it is the sin that lives in me.

Romans 7:19–20 (GNB)

For whatsoever is born of God overcometh the world: and this is the victory that overcometh the world, even our faith. Who is he that overcometh the world, but he that believeth that Jesus is the Son of God?

1 John 5:4–5 (KJV)

These things I have spoken unto you, that in me ye might have peace. In the world ye shall have tribulation: but be of good cheer; I have overcome the world.

John 16:33 (KJV)

'They will fight against you but will not overcome you, for I am with you and will rescue you,' declares the Lord.

Jeremiah 1:19 (NIV)

...for everyone born of God overcomes the world. This is the victory that has overcome the world, even our faith.

1 John 5:4 (NIV)

He that hath an ear, let him hear what the Spirit
saith unto the churches; To him that overcometh
will I give to eat of the tree of life, which is in the
midst of the paradise of God.

Revelation 2:7 (KJV)

He that hath an ear, let him hear what the Spirit
saith unto the churches; He that overcometh shall
not be hurt of the second death.

Revelation 2:11 (KJV)

He that hath an ear, let him hear what the Spirit
saith unto the churches; To him that overcometh
will I give to eat of the hidden manna, and will give
him a white stone, and in the stone a new name
written, which no man knoweth saving he that
receiveth it.

Revelation 2:17 (KJV)

75

And he that overcometh, and keepeth my works
unto the end, to him will I give power over the
nations:

Revelation 2:26 (KJV)

He that overcometh, the same shall be clothed in
white raiment; and I will not blot out his name out
of the book of life, but I will confess his name before
my Father, and before his angels.

Revelation 3:5 (KJV)

Him that overcometh will I make a pillar in the
temple of my God, and he shall go no more out: and
I will write upon him the name of my God, and the
name of the city of my God, which is new
Jerusalem, which cometh down out of heaven from
my God: and I will write upon him my new name.

Revelation 3:12 (KJV)

To him that overcometh will I grant to sit with me
in my throne, even as I also overcame, and am set
down with my Father in his throne.

Revelation 3:21 (KJV)

He that overcometh shall inherit all things; and I
will be his God, and he shall be my son.

Revelation 21:7 (KJV)

In Times of Sickness

And, behold, there was a woman which had a spirit of infirmity eighteen years, and was bowed together, and could in no wise lift up herself.

Luke 13:11 (KJV)

And ye shall serve the Lord your God, and he shall bless thy bread, and thy water; and I will take sickness away from the midst of thee.

Exodus 23:25 (KJV)

For I will restore health unto thee, and I will heal thee of thy wounds, saith the Lord...

Jeremiah 30:17 (KJV)

News about him spread all over Syria, and people brought to him all who were ill with various diseases, those suffering severe pain, the demon-possessed, those having seizures, and the paralysed, and he healed them.

Matthew 4:24 (NIV)

Surely he took up our infirmities and carried our sorrows, yet we considered him stricken by God, smitten by him, and afflicted. But he was pierced for our transgressions, he was crushed for our iniquities; the punishment that brought us peace was upon him, and by his wounds we are healed.

Isaiah 53:4–5 (NIV)

Likewise the Spirit also helpeth our infirmities: for we know not what we should pray for as we ought: but the Spirit itself maketh intercession for us with groanings which cannot be uttered.

Romans 8:26 (KJV)

And he said unto me, My grace is sufficient for thee: for my strength is made perfect in weakness. Most gladly therefore will I rather glory in my infirmities, that the power of Christ may rest upon me. Therefore I take pleasure in infirmities, in reproaches, in necessities, in persecutions, in distresses for Christ's sake: for when I am weak, then am I strong.

2 Corinthians 12:9–10 (KJV)

Is any one of you sick? He should call the elders of the church to pray over him and anoint him with oil in the name of the Lord. And the prayer offered in faith will make the sick person well; the Lord will raise him up. If he has sinned, he will be forgiven.

James 5:14–15 (NIV)

For he hath not despised nor abhorred the affliction of the afflicted; neither hath he hid his face from him; but when he cried unto him, he heard.

Psalm 22:24 (KJV)

To Those Seeking Peace

We hoped for peace but no good has come, for a time of healing but there was only terror.

Jeremiah 8:15 (NIV)

Peace I leave with you; my peace I give you. I do not give to you as the world gives. Do not let your hearts be troubled and do not be afraid.

John 14:27 (NIV)

I have told you these things, so that in me you may have peace. In this world you will have trouble. But take heart! I have overcome the world.

John 16:33 (NIV)

A child is born to us! A son is given to us! And he will be our ruler. He will be called, 'Wonderful Counsellor,' 'Mighty God,' 'Eternal Father,' 'Prince of Peace.'

Isaiah 9:6 (GNB)

It was late that Sunday evening, and the disciples were gathered together behind locked doors, because they were afraid of the Jewish authorities. Then Jesus came and stood among them. 'Peace be with you,' he said.

John 20:19 (GNB)

The mountains and hills may crumble, but my love for you will never end; I will keep forever my promise of peace. So says the Lord who loves you.

Isaiah 54:10 (GNB)

Therefore, since we have been justified through faith, we have peace with God through our Lord Jesus Christ.

Romans 5:1 (NIV)

The mind of sinful man is death, but the mind controlled by the Spirit is life and peace...

Romans 8:6 (NIV)

The Lord gives strength to his people and blesses them with peace.

Psalm 29:11 (GNB)

Be careful for nothing; but in every thing by prayer and supplication with thanksgiving let your requests be made known unto God. And the peace of God, which passeth all understanding, shall keep your hearts and minds through Christ Jesus.

Philippians 4:6–7 (KJV)

83

The peace that Christ gives is to guide you in the
decisions you make...

Colossians 3:15 (GNB)

Of the increase of his government and peace there
will be no end. He will reign on David's throne and
over his kingdom, establishing and upholding it
with justice and righteousness from that time on
and forever. The zeal of the Lord Almighty will
accomplish this.

Isaiah 9:7 (NIV)

...because of the tender mercy of our God, by which
the rising sun will come to us from heaven to shine
on those living in darkness and in the shadow of
death, to guide our feet into the path of peace.

Luke 1:78–79 (NIV)

Concerning the Poor and Needy

'As surely as the Lord your God lives,' she replied, *'I don't have any bread — only a handful of flour in a jar and a little oil in a jug. I am gathering a few sticks to take home and make a meal for myself and my son, that we may eat it — and die.'*

1 Kings 17:12 (NIV)

The Lord your God will bless you in the land that he is giving to you. Not one of your people will be poor...

Deuteronomy 15:4 (GNB)

My whole being will exclaim, 'Who is like you,
O Lord? You rescue the poor from those too strong
for them, the poor and needy from those who rob
them.'

Psalm 35:10 (NIV)

I am weak and poor, O Lord, but you have not
forgotten me. You are my saviour and my God –
hurry to my aid!

Psalm 40:17 (GNB)

Hear, O Lord, and answer me, for I am poor and
needy.

Psalm 86:1 (NIV)

Blessed are the poor in spirit, for theirs is the
kingdom of heaven.

Matthew 5:3 (NIV)

Guard my life, for I am devoted to you. You are my God; save your servant who trusts in you. Have mercy on me, O Lord, for I call to you all day long. Bring joy to your servant, for to you, O Lord, I lift up my soul. You are forgiving and good, O Lord, abounding in love to all who call to you.

Psalm 86:2–5 (NIV)

With my mouth I will greatly extol the Lord; in the great throng I will praise him. For he stands at the right hand of the needy one, to save his life from those who condemn him.

Psalm 109:30–31 (NIV)

Who is like the Lord our God, the One who sits enthroned on high, who stoops down to look on the heavens and the earth? He raises the poor from the dust and lifts the needy from the ash heap; he seats them with princes, with the princes of their people.

Psalm 113:5–9 (NIV)

As it is written: 'He has scattered abroad his gifts to the poor; his righteousness endures forever.'

2 Corinthians 9:9 (NIV)

Listen, my dear brothers: Has not God chosen those who are poor in the eyes of the world to be rich in faith and to inherit the kingdom he promised those who love him?

James 2:5 (NIV)

When in Need of Power

Then Samson prayed, 'Sovereign Lord, please remember me;
please, God, give me my strength just once more…'

Judges 16:28 (GNB)

Lord, there is no one like you; you are mighty, and
your name is great and powerful.

Jeremiah 10:6 (GNB)

But you will receive power when the Holy Spirit
comes on you; and you will be my witnesses in
Jerusalem, and in all Judea and Samaria, and to the
ends of the earth.

Acts 1:8 (NIV)

For to be sure, he was crucified in weakness, yet he lives by God's power. Likewise, we are weak in him, yet by God's power we will live with him to serve you.

2 Corinthians 13:4 (NIV)

I pray that out of his glorious riches he may strengthen you with power through his Spirit in your inner being, so that Christ may dwell in your hearts through faith. And I pray that you, being rooted and established in love, may have power, together with all the saints, to grasp how wide and long and high and deep is the love of Christ...

Ephesians 3:16–18 (NIV)

With this in mind, we constantly pray for you, that our God may count you worthy of his calling, and that by his power he may fulfil every good purpose of yours and every act prompted by your faith.

2 Thessalonians 1:11 (NIV)

The Lord is my strength and my song; he has become my salvation. He is my God, and I will praise him, my father's God, and I will exalt him.

Exodus 15:2 (NIV)

O Lord, be gracious to us; we long for you. Be our strength every morning, our salvation in time of distress.

Isaiah 33:2 (NIV)

He gives strength to the weary and increases the power of the weak. Even youths grow tired and weary, and young men stumble and fall; but those who hope in the Lord will renew their strength. They will soar on wings like eagles; they will run and not grow weary, they will walk and not be faint.

Isaiah 40:29–31 (NIV)

I can do everything through him who gives me strength.

Philippians 4:13 (NIV)

Trust in the Lord. Have faith, do not despair. Trust in the Lord.

Psalm 27:14 (GNB)

But now don't be discouraged, any of you. Do the work, for I am with you... I promised that I will always be with you. I am still with you, so do not be afraid.

Haggai 2:4 (GNB)

Finally, build up your strength in union with the Lord and by means of his mighty power.

Ephesians 6:10 (GNB)

When in Need of Protection

Keep me as the apple of the eye, hide me under the shadow of thy wings, From the wicked that oppress me, from my deadly enemies, who compass me about.

Psalm 17:8–9 (KJV)

The Lord will protect him and preserve his life; he will bless him in the land and not surrender him to the desire of his foes.

Psalm 41:2 (NIV)

'Because he loves me,' says the Lord, 'I will rescue him; I will protect him, for he acknowledges my name.'

Psalm 91:14 (NIV)

My prayer is not that you take them out of the world but that you protect them from the evil one.

John 17:15 (NIV)

But the Lord is faithful, and he will strengthen and keep you safe from the Evil One.

2 Thessalonians 3:3 (GNB)

May the Lord answer you when you are in trouble! May the God of Jacob protect you!

Psalm 20:1 (GNB)

You are my hiding place; you will protect me from trouble and surround me with songs of deliverance.

Psalm 32:7 (NIV)

Yea, though I walk through the valley of the shadow of death, I will fear no evil: for thou art with me; thy rod and thy staff they comfort me.

Psalm 23:4 (KJV)

He that dwelleth in the secret place of the most
High shall abide under the shadow of the Almighty.
I will say of the Lord, He is my refuge and my
fortress: my God; in him will I trust.

Psalm 91:1–2 (KJV)

The Lord shall preserve thee from all evil: he shall
preserve thy soul. The Lord shall preserve thy going
out and thy coming in from this time forth, and
even for evermore.

Psalm 121:7–8 (KJV)

And who is he that will harm you, if ye be followers
of that which is good?

1 Peter 3:13 (KJV)

Regarding God's Providence

And when it was evening, his disciples came to him, saying, This is a desert place, and the time is now past; send the multitude away, that they may go into the villages, and buy themselves victuals. But Jesus said unto them, They need not depart; give ye them to eat. And they say unto him, We have here but five loaves, and two fishes. He said, Bring them hither to me.

Matthew 14:15—18 (KJV)

For the mountains shall depart, and the hills be removed; but my kindness shall not depart from thee, neither shall the covenant of my peace be removed, saith the Lord that hath mercy on thee.

Isaiah 54:10 (KJV)

Consider the lilies how they grow: they toil not, they spin not; and yet I say unto you, that Solomon in all his glory was not arrayed like one of these. If then God so clothe the grass, which is to day in the field, and to morrow is cast into the oven; how much more will he clothe you, O ye of little faith? And seek not ye what ye shall eat, or what ye shall drink, neither be ye of doubtful mind. For all these things do the nations of the world seek after: and your Father knoweth that ye have need of these things. But rather seek ye the kingdom of God; and all these things shall be added unto you.

Luke 12:27–31 (KJV)

Because thou hast made the Lord, which is my refuge, even the most High, thy habitation; There shall no evil befall thee, neither shall any plague come nigh thy dwelling.

Psalm 91:9–10 (KJV)

But my God shall supply all your need according to his riches in glory by Christ Jesus.

Philippians 4:19 (KJV)

About Benjamin he said: 'Let the beloved of the Lord rest secure in him, for he shields him all day long, and the one the Lord loves rests between his shoulders.'

Deuteronomy 33:12 (NIV)

I am the Lord your God, who brought you out of Egypt. Open your mouth, and I will feed you.

Psalm 81:10 (GNB)

In Times of Discouragement

But he himself went a day's journey into the wilderness, and came and sat down under a juniper tree: and he requested for himself that he might die; and said, It is enough; now, O Lord, take away my life; for I am not better than my fathers.

1 Kings 19:4 (KJV)

God is our refuge and strength, a very present help in trouble. Therefore will not we fear, though the earth be removed, and though the mountains be carried into the midst of the sea; Though the waters thereof roar and be troubled, though the mountains shake with the swelling thereof.

Psalm 46:1–3 (KJV)

Though I walk in the midst of trouble, thou wilt revive me: thou shalt stretch forth thine hand against the wrath of mine enemies, and thy right hand shall save me.

Psalm 138:7 (KJV)

If they fall, they will not stay down, because the Lord will help them up.

Psalm 37:24 (GNB)

Cast thy burden upon the Lord, and he shall sustain thee: he shall never suffer the righteous to be moved.

Psalm 55:22 (KJV)

Wait on the Lord: be of good courage, and he shall strengthen thine heart: wait, I say, on the Lord.

Psalm 27:14 (KJV)

The Lord himself goes before you and will be with you; he will never leave you nor forsake you. Do not be afraid; do not be discouraged.

Deuteronomy 31:8 (NIV)

Come unto me, all ye that labour and are heavy laden, and I will give you rest.

Matthew 11:28 (KJV)

Therefore, prepare your minds for action; be self-controlled; set your hope fully on the grace to be given you when Jesus Christ is revealed.

1 Peter 1:13 (NIV)

But he that shall endure unto the end, the same shall be saved.

Matthew 24:13 (KJV)

My brethren, count it all joy when ye fall into divers temptations; Knowing this, that the trying of your faith worketh patience. But let patience have her perfect work, that ye may be perfect and entire, wanting nothing.

James 1:2–4 (KJV)

Why art thou cast down, O my soul? and why art thou disquieted in me? hope thou in God: for I shall yet praise him for the help of his countenance.

Psalm 42:5 (KJV)

Regarding Salvation

When Jesus had lifted up himself, and saw none but the woman, he said unto her, Woman, where are those thine accusers? hath no man condemned thee? She said, No man, Lord. And Jesus said unto her, Neither do I condemn thee: go, and sin no more.

John 8:10–11 (KJV)

Behold, God is my salvation; I will trust, and not be afraid: for the Lord Jehovah is my strength and my song; he also is become my salvation.

Isaiah 12:2 (KJV)

Thou hast also given me the shield of thy salvation: and thy gentleness hath made me great.

2 Samuel 22:36 (KJV)

The Lord liveth; and blessed be my rock; and exalted be the God of the rock of my salvation.

2 Samuel 22:47 (KJV)

But the salvation of the righteous is of the Lord: he is their strength in the time of trouble. And the Lord shall help them, and deliver them: he shall deliver them from the wicked, and save them, because they trust in him.

Psalm 37:39—40 (KJV)

Therefore I will look unto the Lord; I will wait for the God of my salvation: my God will hear me.

Micah 7:7 (KJV)

For the Lord is our judge, the Lord is our lawgiver, the Lord is our king; he will save us.

Isaiah 33:22 (KJV)

She will have a son, and you will name him Jesus —
because he will save his people from their sins.

Matthew 1:21 (GNB)

And then, whoever calls out to the Lord for help
will be saved.

Acts 2:21 (GNB)

Neither is there salvation in any other: for there is
none other name under heaven given among men,
whereby we must be saved.

Acts 4:12 (KJV)

For it is by God's grace that you have been saved
through faith. It is not the result of your own
efforts, but God's gift, so that no one can boast
about it.

Ephesians 2:8–9 (GNB)

When Tired and Weary

And now my soul is poured out upon me; the days of affliction have taken hold upon me. My bones are pierced in me in the night season: and my sinews take no rest.

Job 30:16–17 (KJV)

Come unto me, all ye that labour and are heavy laden, and I will give you rest. Take my yoke upon you, and learn of me; for I am meek and lowly in heart: and ye shall find rest unto your souls. For my yoke is easy, and my burden is light.

Matthew 11:28–30 (KJV)

And he said, My presence shall go with thee, and I will give thee rest.

Exodus 33:14 (KJV)

He maketh me to lie down in green pastures: he leadeth me beside the still waters. He restoreth my soul: he leadeth me in the paths of righteousness for his name's sake.

Psalm 23:2–3 (KJV)

He strengthens those who are weak and tired. Even those who are young grow weak; young men can fall exhausted. But those who trust in the Lord for help will find their strength renewed. They will rise on wings like eagles; they will run and not get weary; they will walk and not grow weak.

Isaiah 40:29–31 (GNB)

My soul finds rest in God alone; my salvation comes from him.

Psalm 62:1(NIV)

Do you not know? Have you not heard? The Lord is the everlasting God, the Creator of the ends of the earth. He will not grow tired or weary, and his understanding no one can fathom. He gives strength to the weary and increases the power of the weak.

Isaiah 40:28–29 (NIV)

For which cause we faint not; but though our outward man perish, yet the inward man is renewed day by day. For our light affliction, which is but for a moment, worketh for us a far more exceeding and eternal weight of glory; While we look not at the things which are seen, but at the things which are not seen: for the things which are seen are temporal; but the things which are not seen are eternal.

2 Corinthians 4:16–18 (KJV)

In Times of Trouble

And Jesus said unto them, See ye not all these things? verily I say unto you, There shall not be left here one stone upon another, that shall not be thrown down. And as he sat upon the mount of Olives, the disciples came unto him privately, saying, Tell us, when shall these things be? and what shall be the sign of thy coming, and of the end of the world?

Matthew 24:2–3 (KJV)

For in the time of trouble he shall hide me in his pavilion: in the secret of his tabernacle shall he hide me; he shall set me up upon a rock.

Psalm 27:5 (KJV)

You are my hiding place; you will protect me from trouble and surround me with songs of deliverance.

Psalm 32:7 (NIV)

But the salvation of the righteous is of the Lord: he is their strength in the time of trouble.

Psalm 37:39 (KJV)

Blessed is he that considereth the poor: the Lord will deliver him in time of trouble.

Psalm 41:1 (KJV)

And call upon me in the day of trouble: I will deliver thee, and thou shalt glorify me.

Psalm 50:15 (KJV)

But I will sing of thy power; yea, I will sing aloud of thy mercy in the morning: for thou hast been my defence and refuge in the day of my trouble.

Psalm 59:16 (KJV)

He will call upon me, and I will answer him; I will be with him in trouble, I will deliver him and honor him.

Psalm 91:15 (NIV)

Then they cried out to the Lord in their trouble, and he delivered them from their distress.

Psalm 107:6 (NIV)

Though I walk in the midst of trouble, thou wilt revive me: thou shalt stretch forth thine hand against the wrath of mine enemies, and thy right hand shall save me.

Psalm 138:7 (KJV)

Alas! for that day is great, so that none is like it: it is even the time of Jacob's trouble; but he shall be saved out of it.

Jeremiah 30:7 (KJV)

Trust in God at all times, my people. Tell him of your troubles, for he is our refuge.

Psalm 62:8 (GNB)

The Lord is good, a refuge in times of trouble. He cares for those who trust in him...

Nahum 1:7 (NIV)

To the Unemployed

But I said, 'I have labored to no purpose; I have spent my strength in vain and for nothing. Yet what is due me is in the Lord's hand, and my reward is with my God.'

Isaiah 49:4 (NIV)

Blessed are all who fear the Lord, who walk in his ways. You will eat the fruit of your labor; blessings and prosperity will be yours. Thus is the man blessed who fears the Lord.

Psalm 128:1–2,4 (NIV)

But my God shall supply all your need according to his riches in glory by Christ Jesus.

Philippians 4:19 (KJV)

May the Lord repay you for what you have done.
May you be richly rewarded by the Lord, the God of
Israel, under whose wings you have come to take
refuge.

Ruth 2:12 (NIV)

Therefore, my dear brothers, stand firm. Let
nothing move you. Always give yourselves fully to
the work of the Lord, because you know that your
labor in the Lord is not in vain.

1 Corinthians 15:58 (NIV)

And God is able to make all grace abound to you, so
that in all things at all times, having all that you
need, you will abound in every good work.

2 Corinthians 9:8 (NIV)

…being confident of this, that he who began a good work in you will carry it on to completion until the day of Christ Jesus.

Philippians 1:6 (NIV)

God is not unjust; he will not forget your work and the love you have shown him as you have helped his people and continue to help them.

Hebrews 6:10 (NIV)

For the Lord your God will bless you in all your harvest and in all the work of your hands, and your joy will be complete.

Deuteronomy 16:15 (NIV)

Commit to the Lord whatever you do, and your plans will succeed.

Proverbs 16:3 (NIV)

The Lord will guide you always; he will satisfy your needs in a sun-scorched land and will strengthen your frame. You will be like a well-watered garden, like a spring whose waters never fail.

Isaiah 58:11 (NIV)

For the sake of his great name the Lord will not reject his people, because the Lord was pleased to make you his own.

1 Samuel 12:22 (NIV)

Now our Lord Jesus Christ himself, and God, even our Father, which hath loved us, and hath given us everlasting consolation and good hope through grace, Comfort your hearts, and stablish you in every good word and work.

2 Thessalonians 2:16–17 (KJV)

In Times of Worry

And it came to pass, that after three days they found him in the temple, sitting in the midst of the doctors, both hearing them, and asking them questions... And when they saw him, they were amazed: and his mother said unto him, Son, why hast thou thus dealt with us? behold, thy father and I have sought thee sorrowing.

Luke 2:46,48 (KJV)

Don't worry about anything, but in all your prayers ask God for what you need, always asking him with a thankful heart. And God's peace which is far beyond human understanding, will keep your hearts and minds safe in union with Christ Jesus.

Philippians 4:6–7 (GNB)

Therefore I tell you, do not worry about your life, what you will eat or drink; or about your body, what you will wear. Is not life more important than food, and the body more important than clothes? Look at the birds of the air; they do not sow or reap or store away in barns, and yet your heavenly Father feeds them. Are you not much more valuable than they? Who of you by worrying can add a single hour to his life?

Matthew 6:25–27 (NIV)

Fret not thyself because of evil men, neither be thou envious at the wicked; For there shall be no reward to the evil man; the candle of the wicked shall be put out.

Proverbs 24:19–20 (KJV)

Be still before the Lord and wait patiently for him;
do not fret when men succeed in their ways, when
they carry out their wicked schemes.

Psalm 37:7 (NIV)

Behold, God will not cast away a perfect man,
neither will he help the evil doers: Till he fill thy
mouth with laughing, and thy lips with rejoicing.

Job 8:20–21 (KJV)

God is our refuge and strength, a very present help
in trouble. Therefore will not we fear, though the
earth be removed, and though the mountains be
carried into the midst of the sea; Though the waters
thereof roar and be troubled, though the mountains
shake with the swelling thereof.

Psalm 46:1–3 (KJV)

The Lord is good, a strong hold in the day of trouble;
and he knoweth them that trust in him.

Nahum 1:7 (KJV)

Cast thy burden upon the Lord, and he shall sustain
thee: he shall never suffer the righteous to be
moved.

Psalm 55:22 (KJV)

I look to the Lord for help at all times, and he
rescues me from danger. Turn to me and be
merciful to me, because I am lonely and weak.
Relieve me of my worries and save me from all my
troubles.

Psalm 25:15–17 (GNB)